# THE DEATH OF SUICIDE!

Destroying the Spirit of Suicide Before it Destroys You!

Paper back    April 2021 ISBN: 978-1-7370827-0-5

Request for information concerning this Manuscript should be sent to the publisher company at

## Make You Free Ministries
P.O Box 494
New York N.Y 10116
www.Makeyoufree.org


Email:Poeticseer@yahoo.com

Revised December 2025

Editor's note: unless otherwise noted in the text, all Scripture quotations are from the Amplified Version by Zondervan Publishing. Used by permission.

**Retail price $ 9.99**

# Table of Contents

# Foreword:

## Plans to Prosper and Not to Harm You

The seven chapters contained in this book are intended not only to bring awareness to the issue of suicide, but to reveal WHO is behind the notion of suicide, and why! This book will also equip you to overcome thoughts of suicide, and to avoid any encounters that could lead you in that direction!

The answers are available to you within these pages; there is no requirement for lengthy programs or self-help groups, no need for medication of any kind! Suicide is an illness that can be cured by one pure and powerful source and remedy that lasts a lifetime! Hundreds of people are senselessly taking their own lives every day, but even one life is too many, because this problem is 100% preventable.

While each of us will face our own mortality one day, it should never be by way of suicide. Enough time has been lost already. What you may not realize is that there is more power available to help you than there is to harm you. All you need to do is take hold of it.

YOU WILL LIVE AND NOT DIE!

*Mark B. Rogers*

# Chapter 1:

## Exposing the Voices

From the very beginning, human beings have offered accounts of hearing strange voices! These voices may disguise themselves as being harmless and coming from someone who cares. They may present themselves as voices of authority, or as messengers of good news with your best interests at heart. These voices may speak eloquently, and they may sound like they offer good ideas. The reality is that words are deadly because the intentions of the person speaking to you have been deadly from the very beginning!

This person has no authority to speak into our lives! We cannot receive our instructions from someone who does not care about us, nor should we take direction from someone who is not responsible for our existence. This makes no earthly sense! If we were created by God (and all the evidence points to this) and placed on the earth by Him, then He alone has the authority to give us our instructions! He alone has the right to tell us what He wants of us, to help us discern right from wrong, and to guide us as to what we should and should not do. Only He can say what would be good and what would be harmful to us, because He is the creator! And he would not create us, only to turn around and give us information that would eventually destroy us. That would be totally illogical because **God is love!**

*"We have come to know [by personal observation and experience], and have believed [with deep, consistent faith] the love which God has for us. **God is love**, and the one who abides in love abides in God, and God abides continually in him."*

--1 John 4:16, emphasis added

When we read the very first two chapters of Genesis, we notice that after hearing how God created the Heavens and the earth, all the galaxies in the universe and all the living creatures, He then goes on to immediately give mankind our instructions!

He gave us the truth, and had we simply listened to what He said, the world would not be in the mess that it is today (and has been in for thousands of years)! Had we listened, we would not have to worry about suicide, or any kind of death, because there would only be life. In this world, life without death is an unimaginable concept, but it is what God had originally intended for His children.

Listen carefully to the instructions given to all by God (and I say, "all" because all of humanity, every culture, and all colors of skin, can be traced back to Adam! Yes, believe it or not, we are all one big human family):

*"And the LORD God commanded the man, saying, "You may freely (unconditionally) eat [the fruit] from every tree of the garden; but [only] from the tree of the knowledge (recognition) of good and evil you shall not eat, otherwise on the day that you eat from it, you shall most certainly die [because of your disobedience]."*--Genesis 2:16-17

So essentially, we were given an open buffet by the Lord, with a simple instruction to not eat from one tree! We were given perfect weather, as evidenced by the fact that no clothing was needed, and perfect food to eat. All the animals were a collection of pets for us to enjoy! Then to top things off, without Adam even asking God for anything, God looked at the man he had created and decided it was not good for him to be alone, so He created Eve, his wife!

*"So, the LORD God caused a deep sleep to fall upon Adam; and while he slept, He took one of his ribs and closed up the flesh at that place. And the rib which the LORD God had taken from the man He made (fashioned, formed) into a woman, and He brought her and presented her to the man."*

--Genesis 2:21-22

This was the voice of our Creator:

He was straightforward and to the point!

His heart and intentions were only good!

After everything He created, He completed His creation with a woman, who would one day become a mother! From Eve would come forth a son and a daughter who would one day be a sister! He wanted us to have a beautiful relationship with Him and with each other! He wanted us to be fruitful and multiply, to keep each other company while enjoying all of God's creation! He wanted us to love and enjoy each other while loving and enjoying

God who made all of it possible! This is the only voice worth listening to! This is the voice of the One who knows what we need before we even ask Him for anything! His is the only voice that matters!

*"For ever since the creation of the world His invisible attributes, His eternal power and divine nature, have been clearly seen, being understood through His workmanship [all His creation, the wonderful things that He has made], so that they [who fail to believe and trust in Him] are without excuse and without defense."*

--Romans 1:20

We should all be able to agree that God did an outstanding job with creation; I would go as far as to describe the universe he created as mind-blowing. It is for this reason that I pause to say, thank you, Heavenly Father, for all that you have done for us!

But then, there came a different voice, one that is smooth and confident, one that is very convincing with words that seem to bring us better news than what we already had. But this is sad, and it troubles me to even think about how completely foolish that sounds! How could anyone offer us more than what we already had? We had **everything!**

The whole earth was ours, and everything in it. We were given dominion over the earth! Most of all, we had God and each other. **Nothing else was needed!** And the icing on the cake was that we had a beautiful relationship with our God, who was responsible for everything that we had.

We were left with no reason at all to listen to any strange voices after receiving the

**B**asic

**I**nstructions

**B**efore

**L**eaving

**E**arth

from the Voice of God!

Examine closely the words of this strange voice and see what it had to say:

*"Now the serpent was more crafty (subtle, skilled in deceit) than any living creature of the field which the LORD God had made. And the serpent (Satan) said to the woman, 'Can it really be that God has said, 'You shall not eat from any tree of the garden'?" And the woman said to the serpent, 'We may eat fruit from the trees of the garden,'"*

--Genesis 3:1-2

Here, we now have a very strange and different voice that has entered the scene. This is the introduction of Satan, otherwise known as the devil. He is a spiritual fallen angel who was kicked out of Heaven:

*"And the great dragon was thrown down, the age-old serpent who is called the devil and Satan, he who continually deceives and seduces the entire inhabited world; he was thrown down to the earth, and his angels were thrown down with him."*

--Revelation 12:9

The devil chose to speak through the snake to Eve because snakes can easily change direction. They have no big bones, only hundreds of little bones wrapped around thousands of muscles. Their curved bodies can move in such a way that you really cannot tell which way they are headed until they stop at their destination. Portions of their body must turn left then right (or vice versa), even when they want to go straight. This was an extremely suitable vessel for Satan's method of operations because he did not want his motives to be known until he achieved his goal!

The devil did not want Eve to think about how strange the words he was speaking really were, and why anyone would even question what God had already told them. The devil was accusing God – who only has a track record of being Good – of somehow mistreating them, of keeping something away from them that they really should have! The devil needed his plans to be totally hidden until he was able to successfully convince Eve to disobey God. And once he deceived her, he was gone! This is shown by the fact that we do not even hear a response from the devil after God pronounces judgement on him.

Every voice which speaks words that contradict the Word of God should not only be looked at as strange, but also as deadly. A voice of this sort should immediately raise eyebrows and suspicion. Let us take a further look at the conversation which transpired between Satan and Eve:

*"And the woman said unto the serpent, we may eat of the fruit of the trees of the garden. **But of the fruit of the tree which is in the midst of the garden, God has said, 'You shall not eat of it, neither shall you touch it, or else you'll die.'** And the serpent said to the woman, you shall not surely die. For God does know that in the day you eat thereof, then your eyes will be opened, and you shall be as gods, knowing good and evil."*

--Genesis 3:2-5, emphasis added

Now we see how Satan slowly built up his attack against Eve's mind to change the desires of her heart with his lies. In verse 1, the devil tries to raise doubt and confusion about what God had said! God never said not to eat of "every" tree in the garden. That is a lie in the form of a question!

We know that Satan's initial plan of attack did not work by Eve's response. She told him what God had said. She also added that the tree should not even be touched, or else she would die! It is only my opinion, but we might infer that these words had been added for effect by Adam in his discussions with Eve, because he wanted to make sure he did not lose the only woman on earth due to her disobedience to God.

Then in verse 4, Satan turns up the attack by unleashing his wickedness in the form of a direct, bold-face lie! He

11

not only told her that she would not die but added emphasis to it by saying "you shall not surely die!" These were the deadliest words ever spoken to a human being, and they came from the voice of the devil, whose name literally means "false accuser." What makes these words deadly is they are calling the holy, pure, and righteous Creator of the universe a liar! God said they would die, and now, the devil is saying they will not. But I am begging you with all my heart to believe me when I say: **God cannot lie!** If He said it, then you can believe it!

*"God is not a man, that he should lie; neither the son of man, that he should repent: hath he said, and shall he not do it? or hath he spoken, and shall he not make it good?"*

--Numbers 23:19 (KJV)

Now, I need you to understand this final, important issue from this chapter; It is vital to your success on earth, and your freedom from the enemy's lies! Though the devil told a grave lie to Eve, a lie itself has no power. You and I are not responsible for someone lying to us. There is no punishment from God if we are lied to by someone else. The lie only becomes harmful and deadly once it is believed! In fact, believing a lie is worse than the lie itself to those who hear it, because a lie that is not believed poses no threat to anyone except to the one who told it on the Day of Judgment:

*"And when the woman saw that the tree was good for food, and that it was pleasant to the eyes, and a tree to be desired to make one wise, she took of the fruit thereof, and*

12

*did eat and gave also unto her husband with her; and he did eat."*        --Genesis 3:6

If a lie is not challenged and resisted, it will marinate like a blend of seasoning soaking into freshly cleaned meat ready to be cooked! After the lie makes a lodging place within us, we ourselves will be cooked and eaten up by the jaws of sin! This is exactly what happened when the lie was not challenged and refuted by Eve. She did eat and furthermore, she gave the fruit to her husband. Not wanting to be separated from his wife, the only woman on earth, Adam ate well!

As a result, they were both cooked! They died spiritually that very same day and began to have evil thoughts and sinful desires to the point they came to see the nakedness of their bodies as something needed to be covered, because their thoughts and desires were infused with both good and evil. They were ashamed of their bodies. They left their sinless nature, a holy and pure state, and exchanged it for our present, sinful nature, which knows what is good but is drawn toward that which is evil.

This all came to pass because Adam and Eve listened and believed the lies that came from the strange and different voice of our adversary, Satan, the arch enemy of all that is good. Unless we recognize there is another voice in this world besides God, a strange voice from a being who knows how to hide behind beauty and appears to mean us well, we too, will be prone to falling for his lies!

Why is all this relevant today? Because that same, strange voice is still causing death all over the world in our day and age:

> ➢ The death of human lives and the death and destruction of everything good in human beings.

> ➢ The death and destruction of homes, of family relationships and marriages.

> ➢ The death and destruction of our health and peace of mind through use of drugs, alcohol, cigarettes and even the overindulgence in food.

Satan's lies are causing chaos, corruption, bitterness, jealousy, envy, hate, racism, misogyny, sexual perversion, confusion, violence, robbery, rape, murder, and **suicide**, just to name a few!

Why is Satan doing this? Jesus said it this way:

*"The **thief** comes only in order to steal and kill and destroy..."*

--John 10:10

Here is the nature and desire of the devil: to steal what does not belong to him, to kill what he did not give life to and to destroy what God has called on to be fruitful and multiply! Satan and his lies are at the root of your

14

problems, which is why this book had to begin with what happened in the beginning!

You must always remember that Satan and his lies are only part of the problem. The fact that we **believe** the lies that come from Satan Is our main problem, and ultimately our downfall which helps our adversary succeed in destroying us.

# Chapter 2.

## Denouncing the Lies

Each of us are lied to all the time! We are lied to through one-on-one encounters with people, be they strangers, co-workers, or classmates. Even family and "friends" will lie to us. However, there are other outlets that pour lies into our minds as well. Have you considered the onslaught of lies in the media? Every day, we are bombarded with messages from TV, Radio, Newspapers, the Internet, and even from billboards! These messages are molding the minds of preschoolers, young children, teenagers, and adults, causing them to think in ways that are harmful to themselves and to others. Here are some examples of the messages we are confronted with every day:

- ➢ Violence is the solution to our problems.

- ➢ The love and pursuit of riches is the most important goal in life.

- ➢ Sex is nothing more than a recreational pastime between two consenting adults.

- ➢ One race is superior to the others.

- ➢ There is no God, so there is no need to fear any judgment for the life you live!

I could fill volumes debunking these lies. However, in this book, we will concentrate on the very first one I mentioned: The notion that "violence is the solution to our problems."

Violence is the intentional use of physical force to cause injury, harm, or damage of various degrees to other people, or to oneself. Now, I will acknowledge that there are some limited cases where violence can be justified. If as a last resort, to protect one's country from its enemies, to defend oneself from an attacker, or to prevent someone from causing harm to others. Other than these limited exceptions, physical violence is not the answer to the problems that we face as adults, or even as young adults. Violence does not correct problems; instead, it usually intensifies them and makes matters worse!

Even an angry outburst not directed at another person is pointless. Suppose a man gets angry and has such uncontrollable rage he feels as though he must punch something. As a result, the man may hit a wall, a door, or another inanimate object. The man may hurt himself or cause damage to whatever he hits, but **the situation that led to his anger did not get better at all.** In fact, we can say with a high degree of confidence that things have become worse. Now, on top of the problem that made him angry to begin with, he has an aching hand and may well have caused damage to someone's property or his own. This is just a small example of how foolish violence is. I can remember acting this way until I learned how to control my anger. I am very thankful to God for all the help He has given me in this area of my life!

None of us would want to have a genuine problem in our lives and respond to the problem in a way that only serves to increase the magnitude of the problem to begin with! This is utter nonsense, which is another way of saying that **it makes no sense at all.** More than anything, we want the problem solved! We want the problem to go away, or at least be headed in that direction.

Who would want to magnify their troubles? Who would want to make matters worse? Who would want to take a small pebble that somehow made its way into the floor of your living room and turn it into a boulder that spreads across the entire living room? Who wants our problems to become more than we can handle? I'll tell you who. It is our adversary, the devil, the same false accuser who spoke through the serpent! The same one who deceived Eve is still here deceiving billions of human beings all over the world, and this book is designed to help expose him and his deceitful ways!

In the Book of Revelation, we read how Satan *"continually deceives and seduces the entire inhabited world,"* (Rev. 12:9). Not only is he responsible for helping to make our small problems worse, he is often responsible for causing so many of our problems to begin with! What makes this reality so harsh is that he knows how to hide under the radar. He knows how to go undetected, to the point where most human beings do not even realize he is there operating under cover in their lives and in their

19

minds. Satan even entered the mind of Judas Iscariot, the disciple who ultimately betrayed Jesus (Luke 22:3-4).

Often, Satan is the invisible hand of evil sitting on the couch in our living rooms. He is planting lies in the theatres through the latest hit at the box office. He is poisoning the minds of children through the graphic images they see on the Internet, and through the profane music they listen to on their electronic devices. He may have started off by speaking through the serpent in the time of Adam and Eve, but he has quickly learned how to speak through the human beings he enters! And he makes it his business to communicate with us through the misuse of technology!

The reason Satan can cover so much ground is because he does not act alone. Scripture tells us there are millions and millions of other fallen angels, spirits he has taken captive to carry out his evil agenda. He has a veritable empire of evildoers who work closely together in the spiritual realm, (a network whose power and effectiveness would be the envy of any organized crime syndicate.) **In fact, it would be no exaggeration to call Satan and his minions the largest and longest running terrorist organization in the world!** However, these terrorists will not get away with their crimes against Humanity and their rebellion against God, for they have already been judged, convicted, and sentenced to eternal damnation in hell!

*"Then shall he say also unto them on the left hand, 'Depart from me, ye cursed, into everlasting fire, **prepared for the devil and his angels.'"***

--Matthew 25:41 (KJV), emphasis added

They have not all gone to hell, yet! Only some of them:

*"For if God spared not the angels that sinned, **but cast them down to hell, and delivered them into chains of darkness, to be reserved unto judgment ...**"*

--2 Peter 2:4 (KJV), emphasis added

The rest of them are here, roaming the atmosphere seeking whomever they can swallow up:

*"Be sober, be vigilant; because your adversary the devil, as a roaring lion, walketh about, seeking whom he may devour:"*

--1 Peter 5:8 (KJV)

Look at how the Apostle Paul describes the devil:

*"You were following the ways of this world [influenced by this present age], in accordance with the prince of the power of the air (Satan), the spirit who is now at work in the disobedient [the unbelieving, who fight against the purposes of God]."*        --Ephesians 2:2

Evil thoughts can enter a human mind, changing your mood, your feelings, and ultimately, your decisions (read Acts 5:3). Because you cannot see them, you will not realize what has happened Until your eyes are spiritually opened, you will assume these thoughts originated within you!

**Out of Sight, Not Out of Mind:**

Evil spirits are clever at staying hidden, and they hate being exposed and revealed in any way. They even hate that this book is exposing them! Why? Because once you find out who they are and what they are up to, you will want to search out the answer to overcome them, which I will explain in the following chapters.

Demons are clever beings who cunningly know how to put together strategies to further their agenda. The biggest lie that has flooded our society is when those who are suffering from demonic possession are diagnosed as people simply suffering from mental illness!

As long as the problem is viewed as strictly a mental one they will only medicate the body, and totally avoid the spiritual condition which is the core of the problem! If no spiritual assessment and application is initiated, demonic influences go unaddressed. While the human body may be medicated (and the tendency toward violent behavior slowed down as a result) the underlying problem does not go away. It remains just below the surface, ready to rear its ugly head again once the medication wears off!

As a person becomes familiar with those strange demonic voices loaded with subtle lies, it becomes natural to listen to them, and to claim them as their own. Over time, the instructions become louder and clearer, to the point of death – whether it is the death of someone else, the death of self, or both! It will always somehow lead to death!

**Staggering Statistics!**

I will not bore you with tons of facts and figures, but I do think it is important to offer examples from a few countries so that you can see just how serious this issue has become globally:

In **Australia**, these are the number of suicides that took place over a recent three-year period:

3,128 in 2017

3,138 in 2018

3,318 in 2019

This means an average of nine people are dying by suicide each day in Australia.

Although the rate of suicide has decreased somewhat in **Canada**, the numbers are nevertheless very troubling:

4,157 in 2017

3,811 in 2018

4,012 in 2019

Suicide rates also remain stubbornly high in **England and Wales**:

5,821 in 2017

5,420 in 2018

5,691 in 2019

In the United States, suicide rates have risen consistently over the past twenty years. Here are the statistics for the three years current data is available:

47,173 committed suicide in 2017

48,344 committed suicide in 2018

47,511 committed suicide in 2019

Even more shocking are the number of people who have **attempted** suicide and failed. In 2019 alone, there were 1,380,000 suicide attempts! Suicide is now the 10th leading cause of death in America, with an average of 132 suicides daily, roughly half of which are the result of self-inflicted gunshot wounds.

Many other countries are suffering from this epidemic as well. But what makes these jaw-dropping statistics even harder to digest is these tragedies were 100% preventable. Not some of them, but all of them! This is a crisis that deserves far more attention than it has been receiving in the media. As I stated previously, while it is true that we all must die, we do not have to lose our lives to suicide!

The idea that suicide provides a way out of our suffering is a lie, fabricated by the father of lies. There is no problem any human being faces that is made better by taking one's own life! The same voices that have led millions to molest, rape, rob, and murder are leading thousands to kill themselves. This is the work of the devil and his demons, who could care less about our well-being!

> They are the ones who have led humanity into making many horrible and regrettable decisions.

> They are the ones who have led you to do things that now fill you with shame, things that you never thought you were capable of doing.

> They are the ones that have falsely accused God by convincing you that He is to blame for your personal situation and that God does not love you!

> They are the ones that have told men to rape and violate women!

> They are the ones that have led men to molest little children as young as four years of age, and that have managed to convince those men that the pleasure they will receive is worth it!

> They are the ones that have led millions to take a coco plant or the buds of marijuana and smoke it in pursuit of a temporary pleasurable feeling while killing the very brain cells they used to obtain it!

> They are the ones that told men to take the seed pod of various opium plants and turn it into morphine, then turn that into heroin, cook it, then sniff it or inject it into their bodies! All this just to obtain more pleasure at the risk of damaging their health and possibly causing a heart attack!

Let me be clear: **no human being would think of doing these awful things on their own. It is not natural!** And they are the ones who have been telling you that nobody cares about you, that your life is worthless and that you would be better off dead.  But these are all lies.

**You are most certainly not better off dead!**

- ➤ You are better off alive and having all your sins forgiven.

- ➤ You are better off with the Lord fighting your battles.

- ➤ You are better off having your spiritual eyes opened, so that you can plainly see who is behind the curtain pulling the strings of billions of minds without them knowing it.

- ➤ You are better off with the life-changing power of the Holy Spirit working within you.

- ➤ You are better off with the devil permanently banished from your life.

- ➤ You are better off overcoming the lying voices and thoughts of suicide by the power and strength of the Lord God almighty, who wants you to live and have the victory!

In This way you can and will go on to have success in your life. Success with your family. Success in your marriage. Success in your single life until you are married. Success in your job or your business. Success in your physical and spiritual health. And most importantly, success in your personal relationship with your Creator!

These are all very present and real options, and this is the opportunity that awaits you.

These are the words that must be believed.

These are the words that will bring deliverance to you!

Believing these words will not only deliver you, but it will also equip you to be a spokesperson to go out and help deliver others who are struggling with the wicked, foolish, and lying voices that plant thoughts of suicide in them!

Of course, the adversary would never tell you such things because that would be telling you the truth, which is something he cannot do. Jesus rebuked those who refused to believe the Good News which He came to offer:

*"You are of your father the devil, and the lusts of your father you will do. He was a murderer from the beginning, and abode not in the truth, because there is no truth in him. **When he speaks a lie, he speaks of his own: for he is a liar, and the father of it."***

--John 8:44 (KJV), emphasis added

None of the enemy's thoughts can be fabricated by humans on their own! Those thoughts are all unnatural!

In other words, there is nothing within a human body born into this world that would have a desire for those things at all. For the most part, all human beings basically have the same desires when we come into the world; we want to eat, to play, to remain in a healthy environment free from physical pain and suffering, to dwell in safety and comfort, to have companionship, and to safely enjoy pleasure without bringing harm to ourselves or to others.

These are the things a normal human being wants!

The only way humans end up deviating from these thoughts are when their minds are being deceived by intruders who have entered in without permission and are not being ordered to leave!

**Intruder Alert**!

If anyone enters our home without permission, we confront them immediately. And if we are frightened, we call the police as well! We would never allow someone unknown to us to intrude our homes without confronting and stopping them! We would not take the time to engage them in a discussion and find out what they wanted; we would just want them out of our home and punished for breaking and entering our private living space!

**How much more should we have this same attitude toward fallen evil spirits that do not belong within us?**

Jesus tells us that this enemy is a thief (John 10:10), so we know that these spirits are coming to take something that does not belong to them. But what exactly do they want?

What are they trying to take from us? There are three things they are after:

> First, they want to take over your mind! If anyone can control your mind, they can and will control your life!

> Second, once they gain control of your mind, they want to cause as much chaos and destruction in the lives of as many other people as possible through you! Perhaps you have seen people like this, and they are precisely whom you should steer clear of!

> Third, they ultimately want to destroy you once they are finished and have no more use for you!

This will always be their agenda, like Jesus said.

Yes, as human beings we are easily influenced! Our minds can be intruded upon with wicked thoughts we did not ask for, all by an unseen enemy we never knew. The devil and his demons have been using the very same tactics to destroy us since the beginning of mankind. Their lies are dressed up to seem pleasing and harmless. They trap us in a cage of sin, torment, and agony. We suffer excruciating pain and ultimately death. All in the name of fame, pleasure, and oftentimes, both. We need to be aware of their voices and see them for the intruders they are!

We need to view them as unwelcome guests in our minds who must be commanded to leave. What you allow to take root in your mind, you will ultimately believe. Such harmful thoughts must be shown the door!

**You must come to recognize these thoughts as being separate from you.** The world does not realize that not all thoughts reflect who you are! Evil spirits do not want you to know this because being aware of the truth and denouncing them is the start of your victory!

**Denounce and Reject**!

Now that we see lies are only effective once believed and acted upon, what would happen if you chose not to believe them? What if you chose to adamantly reject them and considered them to be a poisonous and a deadly waste of time? What if you chose to believe the truth about who you are in the eyes of the One who made you? How much power would the enemy have over you? How much destruction and damage could the enemy cause in our lives, our families, and our homes? The answer is **None!**

For this reason, it is crucial that we replace these lies with the Truth. If not, we will become frustrated and annoyed by the decisions we make, because these decisions will spring forth from the fountain of lies! You will not hear about this in polite company, because the god of this world (who is Satan) has blinded the minds of those who do not believe the truth (2 Corinthians 4:4)

**The key to the problem of suicide, and to all other destructive thoughts a person will ever have, is to become aware of where deceitful ideas come from, and to denounce and reject the author of these lies!**

We were not designed to live under demonic influence and believe the enemy's lies! They do not belong within us and must be told to leave immediately. You will always be "out of order" and never live out the life you were intended to live so long as your life is built on lies!

**There is something of even greater importance that must be done right away. Once you tell the lying voices to leave, you must immediately replace those lies with the Truth! Your mind was not meant to be devoid of any thoughts, and it needs the Truth to guard against the lies from reentering. God's truth will empower you!**

# Chapter 3

# What Does God Have to Say About Suicide?

It is important to know what the heart of our Creator has to say about the subject of suicide, and about death in general. So, we will now turn our attention to a few statements from the Bible, which is the Word of God Himself:

*"And God blessed them, and God said unto them, 'Be fruitful, and multiply, and replenish the earth, and subdue it: and have dominion over the fish of the sea, and over the fowl of the air, and over every living thing that moves upon the earth.'"*

--Genesis 1:28 (KJV)

Here we have the first recorded statement God makes to mankind concerning life, and His instructions were simply to be fruitful and multiply! **In essence, God is saying, "continue this life that I have given you, and keep producing life!"**

God's promises, as well as His commandments, are embodied in the "covenants" He makes with His people. Later, while establishing a covenant relationship with the children of Israel and giving them warnings of what could happen to them if they were to disobey, God places emphasis on what He wants from them:

*"I call heaven and earth to record this day against you, that I have set before you life and death, blessing and cursing: therefore, choose life, that both thou and thy seed may live."*

--Deuteronomy 30:19 (KJV)

Pay careful attention to what God says here. Not only does He say to "choose life," so that **you** can live, but He adds, **"that both you and your children may live."**

On another occasion many years later, we get a clear picture of how God feels about the wicked and what He wants them to do:

*"But if the wicked will turn from all his sins that he has committed, and keep all my statutes, and do that which is lawful and right, he shall surely live, he shall not die."*

--Ezekiel 18: 21 (KJV)

Just to know this is the kind of heart that God has for those who have gone astray should be extremely comforting to us, because **whether we want to admit it or not, we have all done wicked things**. But He said if we turn from our sins and begin to keep His statutes, we will "surely live and not die!"

In the very same book, God goes one step further and exposes His heart's desire through His servant Ezekiel, saying this:

*"Say unto them, As I live, says the Lord GOD, I have no pleasure in the death of the wicked; but that the wicked turn from his way and live: turn now, turn now from your evil ways; for why will ye die, O house of Israel? "*

--Ezekiel 33:11 (KJV)

By now, it should become clear to you that God takes no pleasure at all in the death of the wicked. None! His desire is for us to be redeemed. This means that we cannot allow our past sinful behavior to keep us from God today. Instead, we must turn from those ways and live! And God places emphasis on the word "turn" by saying it twice! He then asks rhetorically, "why will you die, O house of Israel?" It does not get any plainer than that!

This is coming from the highest authority in the universe. It is a powerful question that He asks, and we can apply this to everyone, because God is Love and He loves all just as He loved the house of Israel!

Now, put your name in the same question God is now asking you! "WHY WILL YOU DIE _____?

**Why would you die when your Creator gets no pleasure from it at all, and he would much rather you just turn from your wicked ways and live?**

Here is what king Solomon, one of the wisest men to ever walk the earth, has to say about taking heed of the laws of God! Listen to what God led him to write:

*"My son, forget not my law; but let your heart keep my commandments. For length of days, and long life, and peace, shall they add to you."*

--Proverbs 3:1, 2 (KJV)

Can you see God's consistent desire being expressed to us? We are being told if we listen to the laws of God, the "length of days" which means long life, will be given to us. And to make sure we understand this will not be a life of torment, He adds peace. It cannot be made any clearer than this! There is not even the slightest suggestion from God almighty through His Word that he desires death for us, let alone death by suicide!

In case we need reminding, God our creator not only knows how to make life, but to take lives when necessary. When He has determined that a person's time should be up, and for whatever reason He deems, God will end that person's life. Listen to something He has said about life and death:

*"See now that I, even I, am He, and there is no god with Me: **I kill, and I make alive**; I wound, and I heal: neither is there any that can deliver out of My hand."*

--Deuteronomy 32:39 (KJV)

While the Lord was warning Israel, He had to be sure to remind them that He had the power to kill and make alive! I share this with you now so that you can understand that if God ever wanted to take your life, He does not need your help or permission. He can do it all by himself.

36

And if you are still alive after all that you have been through, it is because He **wants** you to remain alive!

And finally, I need to show you how Jesus expresses the same exact heart as God the Father! Listen to what He said when He uses a comparison between Himself and the devil as to the reasons why each of them will enter a person's life:

*"The thief comes only in order to steal, and to kill, and to destroy; I have come that they might have life, and that they might have it more abundantly."*

--John 10:10 (KJV)

Now we see that Jesus not only wants us to have life, but to have an abundant life! Abundant in what, you might ask? Abundant in love, joy, and peace! Abundant in wisdom, abundant in discernment to know good from evil! Abundant in understanding of spiritual warfare and how to avoid the foolish traps of the enemy! Abundant in everything that is good.

# Chapter 4

## Accepting the Truth

Many have asked this question concerning the fall with the serpent and Eve: if God knew that Eve would listen to the serpent, why did He not intervene? Why did He leave them there to deal with the lies of the serpent alone?

The answer is that God had already given Adam and Eve everything they needed to overcome all the lies that could have ever come from Satan's mouth. God had given them the truth, and the truth was all they needed to slam the door in the face of the devil. Believing lies only enslaves us to a life a sin and death. We end up living a life we were never intended to live, and even when we realize what we are doing is wrong, it is hard for us to stop!

The usage of cigarettes provides a great illustration of this concept. Kids will listen to the lie, often repeated by their peers, that smoking is cool and something which they need to do to be accepted and even respected amongst their peers. And because many of us badly want to be accepted, and not seen as an outcast, we end up giving in to the idea! This is how people become trapped by their addiction to nicotine, and then years later they are still engaging in this destructive behavior that sabotages their finances and their health in exchange for fleeting pleasure! Tobacco usage is responsible for 480,000 deaths; that is about 1,300 deaths a day. And that's not mentioning other countries like the UK, Canada, Australia our the many countries in Asia, Africa and Europe and it all starts from being pressured to believe the Lie that smoking is cool and will make you accepted by your peers!

This is just one of many vices for which the father of lies is responsible. Here is a list of some others:

➢ Drugs

➢ Alcohol

➢ Sexual immorality in all its forms

➢ The love of money

➢ The pursuit of fame

➢ The hunt for pleasure,

➢ The belief that there is no God, or that if God exists, you do not need Him, or can redefine Him to fit your own lifestyle.

I could go on … and the reason the enemy has so many types of lies is because he knows we are all different, and we will not be taken in by every lie. With such a wide variety of falsehoods, he knows that even if you are wise enough not to fall for one, you will fall for another!

You can pick and choose any lie that appeals to you, and it will trap you and make you a slave to it. With each lie, there is an evil spirit whose goal is to reinforce the lie within you and have you act upon it. Even when a person realizes the lifestyle they have chosen is too harmful to live with, they no longer have the power to stop living under a lie which they should have never chosen to believe in the first place!

Then the reality of being powerless begins to take its toll on the individual. They adopt a defeatist attitude, because they believe there is no answer to the problems of this life. Along comes another demon to bring a last lie into their minds as the final "solution" to their problem: **the lie of suicide!**

No sane human being would ever throw something away of great value, including themselves! Satan leads us to live in a manner which leaves us empty and spiritually bankrupt, and this will also lead us to conclude that our own lives are worthless. This is how he goes about convincing us to throw our lives away! The kingdom of darkness has been instructed by the devil himself to push you to believe that this is your best option, hoping that you do not come across the real answer!

Satan's objective is to keep you and I in bondage until the day we die, and all the while these lies bring curses upon our lives and upon our homes and families. Many times, they create generational curses, where parents pass down the chaos of their lives to their children, only to have them repeat the cycle!

**Breaking the Bondage**:

How can the bondage of sin be broken, since believing these lies got us into this mess to begin with? How can these chains of sin be removed from our minds so that our thoughts can be pure, and our behavior become clean? It is by embracing the Truth, the Word of God. The answer will always lead us back to God the creator because his Word is the Truth and has power within it. The Word of God has the power to renew the human mind, to free us from bondage and to change lives!

You may be wondering why God's truth alone provides us with the power we need as human beings. As I stated earlier, the truth is inherently connected to God! He is one with His thoughts and His word. Therefore, truth exclusively belongs to Him! And He is the most powerful being that has ever and will ever be in the universe. The Word of God is life-changing because we innately know within our being that truth comes from our Creator! When we finally embrace the truth, that which is right for us and for all people, there is a joy associated with it! We sense a great level of inner peace!

God's truth is a shield which cannot be penetrated because it is the very Word of God! God's voice is so powerful that when He speaks, things are brought forth into being. When God spoke, the crust, the mantel, the soil, and the core of the earth began to exist. The rocks and the mountains began to form. Waters gathered in one place to form the ocean and the seas. The sun, the moon, and the stars all took their place in the sky and remain where they are told to this day. All by the voice of God!

*"For the word of God is living and active and full of power [making it operative, energizing, and effective]. It is sharper than any two-edged sword, penetrating as far as the division of the soul and spirit [the completeness of a person], and of both joints and marrow [the deepest parts of our nature], exposing and judging the very thoughts and intentions of the heart."*

--Hebrews 4:12

His Word is alive and active and is like medicine to our souls. Once heard and believed in its fullness, the Word of God will bring new life to that person. It will cause lies to dissipate and the bondage which they have endured to be shattered and broken into pieces. His word is powerful; powerful enough to destroy that which is evil while at the same time preserving us, the ones who God desires to love and to offer abundant life!

So, seeing that God is in our favor and that He has our best interest at heart, we would be wise to allow the power of His Word to put to death every single evil thought within us that needs to die, especially the death of suicide! And once God destroys the stronghold of the enemy's lies, we are now at liberty to live freely. However, this does not come to us from merely "hearing" the truth, but from believing it and personally knowing it to be true. For this reason, Jesus told those who were slaves to sin:

*"And ye shall know the truth, and the truth shall make you free."*

--John 8:32 (KJV)

Free from what?

> ➤ Free from the bondages of sin.

> ➤ Free from a life of torment and anguish.

> ➤ Free from sexual perversion.

> ➤ Free from substance abuse.

> ➤ Free from loving money.

> ➤ Free from the pursuit of pleasure.

> ➤ Free from a life of fear.

> ➤ Free from speaking and believing lies.

> ➤ Free from hatred and racism.

> ➤ Free from violence and murder.

> ➤ Free from perverted lustful thoughts.

And last but certainly not least:

> ➤ Free from thoughts of suicide!

And because the Word of God is life-sustaining, this is exactly why Jesus said:

*"It is written and forever remains written, 'man shall not live by bread alone, **but by every word that comes out of the mouth of God.**"*

--Mathew 4:4, emphasis added

The Word of God should be precious to us. The Lord had His Word written down and preserved for us until this day, knowing that it would accomplish the good work which He had set out to do in us!

*"So will My word be which goes out of My mouth; It will not return to Me void (useless, without result), without accomplishing what I desire, and without succeeding in the matter for which I sent it. "*

--Isaiah 55:11

You might find this hard to imagine, but I was once someone who did not believe the Bible! I thought all I needed to do in life was to make money, and that would bring me everything my heart desired. In doing so, I made money my god! It took me some years of pain and suffering to realize that money cannot buy love, it cannot buy joy, and it cannot buy peace. And I have since learned that **no human being was created to live without love, joy, and peace within them!**

Living a life without these attributes is a set up for disaster! **It is why many have committed suicide already**! So many men and women could not withstand the torment and misery, or the various bondages of wickedness! It is frustrating to us when we live like that, because in our hearts we know it is not right even if we enjoy it!

**Today is the day of Salvation!**

But from this moment onwards, you will experience the freedom God wants you to have!
You will enjoy the abundant life that Christ Jesus said He wants you to live.
You will allow the Lord God almighty to kick the devil out of your life and take all his lies with him.
You will live and not die!
You will become exactly who God wants you to become!
And even if you do not have the supportive friends and family you need, God will bring them into your life at the right time!

But first, it is time for us to take a break from reading and say a prayer of confession and repentance right now! Because this is what the Lord is waiting for!

Before we pray, you must first understand who Jesus is and why He is important to know to obtain the salvation of the Lord and come to the truth!

*"For this is good and acceptable in the sight of God our Savior, who will have all men to be saved, and to come unto the knowledge of the truth. **For there is one God, and one mediator between God and mankind, the man Christ Jesus, who gave himself a ransom for all, to be testified in due time.**"*

--1 Timothy 2:3-6 (KJV), emphasis added

The truth is that we have all fallen short, and none of us are right with God. Left to our own devices, none of us could have the kind of relationship Adam and Eve once had with God, however brief it may have been! Our sinful nature keeps us away from Him as we seek to serve and please ourselves. But Jesus is the mediator who brings us back to God! He is the bridge that takes us out of darkness into the Kingdom of light! Because God is holy and just, He demands a punishment for sinful deeds. But because He loves us so much, He did not want us to receive the punishment we deserve. This is the reason He sent Jesus to be the sacrificial Lamb of God, who would take the punishment for sin upon Himself in our place!

*"For God so loved the world, that he gave his only begotten Son, that whosoever believeth in him should not perish, but have everlasting life.* **For God sent not his Son into the world to condemn the world; but that the world through him might be saved.***"

--John 3:16-17 (KJV), emphasis added

Now, because Jesus paid the penalty for our sins, all human beings need to do is simply and genuinely believe in Him and confess Him as the Lord over your life!

*"Because if you acknowledge and confess with your mouth that Jesus is Lord [recognizing His power, authority, and majesty as God], and believe in your heart that God raised Him from the dead, you will be saved. For with the heart a person believes [in Christ as Savior] resulting in his justification [that is, being made righteous--being freed of the guilt of sin and made acceptable to God]; and with the mouth he acknowledges*

47

and confesses [his faith openly], resulting in and confirming [his] salvation."

--Romans 10:9-10

**And lastly:**

*"And we have seen and do testify that the Father sent the Son to be the Savior of the world."*

--1 John 4:14 (KJV)

Now that it is clear to you who Jesus is, here is a prayer you can pray if you are ready to receive forgiveness of sins and the salvation of the Lord through Jesus!

*"Heavenly Father, I confess that I am a sinner in need of a Savior.*

*"I believe that you sent Jesus to be the Savior of the World, and that He paid the price for my sins. I also believe that He rose from the dead by you, which shows that you were pleased with His sacrifice!*

*"I now turn from my sinful lifestyle and I ask that Jesus become the Lord and Savior of my life!*

*"Give me your Holy Spirit and lead me every day of my life!"*

*In Jesus' name I pray! Amen*

If you prayed this prayer and meant it, then you have now received the salvation of the Lord! God has spiritually made you a brand- new person!

*"Therefore, if anyone is in Christ [that is, grafted in, joined to Him by faith in Him as Savior], he is a new creature [reborn and renewed by the Holy Spirit]; the old things [the previous moral and spiritual condition] have passed away. Behold, new things have come [because spiritual awakening brings a new life]."*

--2 Corinthians 5:17

Now that you are a new person at heart, there is something you must know! There is something else which you were given, something which comes along with the "package" of salvation which you just accepted, and that is the power of the Holy Spirit! The Lord Jesus has given you, and all His followers, power over our enemy!

*"Behold!* ***I have given you authority and power to trample upon serpents and scorpions****, and [physical and mental strength and ability] over all the power that the enemy [possesses]; and nothing shall in any way harm you.* ***Nevertheless, do not rejoice at this, that the spirits are subject to you but rejoice that your names are enrolled in heaven."***

--Luke 10: 19-20, emphasis added

This is excellent news! Not only are we forgiven of our sins, but we have been given power over the enemy! We now have power over the invisible, evil spirits that have

49

been influencing and tormenting us for years! This power is needed because we will still have to engage with this enemy, even though it has been removed from our lives. Just because he has been removed does not mean he will leave us alone! But now it no longer matters! Because you now have everything you need to live an abundant and victorious life. You have both the power of His Word to make full use of and cleanse your mind and purify your thoughts, as well as the indwelling presence and power of the Holy Spirit of God!

You are now fully equipped to take on any spiritual battle, because Jesus will now fight those battles with you! The One who has all power and authority under His command will never leave you:

*"And Jesus came and spake to them, saying,* ***'all power is given to me in heaven and in earth.*** *Go therefore, and teach all nations, baptizing them in the name of the Father, and of the Son, and of the Holy Ghost; teaching them to observe all things whatsoever I have commanded you:* ***and, lo, I am with you always, even to the end of the world. Amen.***"

--Mathew 28:18-20 (KJV), emphasis added

# Chapter 5

# The Victory Achieved

The biggest and most dangerous lies used are lies which have pieces of the truth within them! This tactic has been used successfully by the enemy in getting us to believe him for thousands of years. He is a master at speaking partial truths. You should always be cautious of this approach. Be extremely suspicious when it appears something is being left out, **because a partial truth is the equivalent of a full lie!**

We were designed by God to operate in the full truth, not in partial truths infused and merged with lies. Here are some popular examples:

➢ He will take something that you did **(True)**

➢ And then say because you did this thing, you are a failure and should no longer live **(Not true)**

➢ He will take the fact that you do not look attractive in someone's eyes **(True)**

➢ And then tell you that you could never be attractive in anyone's eyes **(Not true)**

➢ He will take the fact that a group of people made fun of you **(True)**

- ➤ And then convince you that no one will ever like you and that people will always make fun of you **(Not true)**

- ➤ He will even take the bad circumstances into which you may have been born into **(True)**

- ➤ And then say, "because of that, you can never amount to anything good" **(Not True)**

Or worse,

- ➤ He may tell you that because of those circumstances, that shows you God does not love you or care about you **(Not true)**

Or worse still,

- ➤ He may tell you that because of those circumstances that gave you a difficult start in life, you are better off dead because your life is not worth living **(Not true)**

But none of those things matter now: I repeat:

**It doesn't matter!**

Your past cannot define your future because the Lord God has already decided upon your future! He said this:

*But you are a chosen generation, a royal priesthood, a holy nation, a peculiar people; that you should shew forth the praises of him who has **called you out of darkness into his marvelous light.** "*

--1 Peter 2:9 (KJV)

And you must say of yourself what king David said of himself when praying to God:

*"I will praise you; for I am fearfully and wonderfully made; marvelous are your works; and that my soul knows very well."*

--Psalm 139:14 (KJV)

Sure, you may have done some bad and despicable things in darkness; we all have! But you are no longer in darkness. You have been called out of darkness and into His marvelous light!

Sure, you may not look the exact same way as others do, but you are still beautiful, because everyone God has ever created was and is beautiful! It is only sin, acted out and displayed, that is ugly in anyone and Everyone! It does not matter what you have done, or how many times you may have done it. None of this has taken God by surprise! Although He did not approve of it, He was not shocked by it. He knew you were prone to doing these things, and because He loves you, He has provided a way of escape for you from your life of sin!

He made it so that there would be a window of opportunity for you to not only be forgiven for your wicked behavior, but He has also provided a way to empower you to live a life where you would not have to repeat those same wicked acts!

His voice is the highest authority! His decisions cannot be overruled or overturned! And therefore, His voice is the only one that matters ... and He said that you should live!

So, when the strange voice of the enemy reminds you of the wicked things you have done, remind him that you have been forgiven. For it is written:

*"If we confess our sins, **he is faithful and just to forgive us of our sins,** and to cleanse us from all unrighteousness."*

--1 John 1:9 (KJV), emphasis added

And because you are forgiven, you face no condemnation by God! It is also written:

*"There is therefore now **no condemnation to them which are in Christ Jesus**, who walk not after the flesh, but after the Spirit."*

--Romans 8:1 (KJV)

This means you do not have to worry about being punished by God for all the things you've done wrong! You will not be condemned for it because we have confessed your sins to Him, and you are now in Christ ... meaning that we have made an agreement to submit to His Lordship, and to His Person. So, when we are looked upon by our Heavenly Father, God sees His Son Jesus!

The condemning lies which the devil uses that still work on many people will no longer work on you and me ...

We know exactly where we stand! God loves us so much He wants us to be victorious on earth! And through Jesus, we have been given the victory!

*"but thanks be to God, who gives us the victory [as conquerors] through our Lord Jesus Christ. "*

--1 Corinthians 15:57

Millions of people are still lost! Billions do not know the truth that there is liberty found in the Gospel of Jesus Christ and by believing the good news, the truth of God's word! So, they continue to live defeated lives ... overwhelmed and trampled on by the powers of darkness!

And what makes this such a sad reality is when you try to bring this beautiful, life-saving truth to people many reject this news and just say, "No, thank you. That can't be the answer that I'm looking for."

**In actuality, it is not only the answer that they are looking for, but it is the only answer there is!**

So, when people say that "I want nothing to do with Christ or Christianity," they may not realize it, but they are really saying, "I do not want power over my enemies, Satan and the many evil spirits that exist. I want to fight my own spiritual battles against demons that are thousands of years old and are more clever and stronger than I am! And I don't want any help from God at all!"

And when I encounter people like this, I shake my head and immediately make a mental note to keep them in my prayers, hoping one day, the Lord will show them the error of their ways before it is too late!

# Chapter 6

## The Fight Will Continue!

You and I have been given free will to exercise as we see fit. We were also given moral laws that were written upon our hearts from birth. But what you may not know is although you are accountable for your own actions, your mind is also open for public inspection in the spirit realm, so to speak! This means at any given time, your mind can be visited by a spirit that brings along with it a specific thought … or thoughts!

At this point, these spirits are powerless over you, depending on what you do at this moment. They can only bring an idea or suggestion to you, but that is as far as they can go unless you give them more control. And that is what happens when the thought is not challenged and removed!

If that negative thought takes up residence in your mind, it will begin to transform into a feeling in your body! And that feeling, if not suppressed and resisted, will become an action! That action will then take shape and mold your character, easing its way into your lifestyle over time. And that lifestyle will bring you to your destiny … all because the thought was never dealt with appropriately in the first place!

We have all encountered these kinds of battles in our minds throughout our lives. Many have already committed suicide as a result, and some have even murdered others and many have done all kinds of unspeakable acts. Some are still struggling with all sorts of evil thoughts that they just cannot seem to shake.

There is a way to have complete victory in this area; there is power available to win these fights. This is something billions of people on the earth do not know! And equally important is after hearing the true reality of "Spiritual Warfare 101," the person would still need the spiritual power of the Lord to be able to fend off the attacks and spiritually discern whether a thought is simply their own fears and concerns, or a visitation from the evil one!

Either way, the word of God makes it clear what all servants must do with inappropriate thoughts. When you have time, you can read the entire text of Paul's second letter to the Church in Corinth, but for now, I just want to focus on spiritual warfare in the mind and the handling of ungodly thoughts the right way:

*"For though we walk in the flesh, we do not war after the flesh: (for the weapons of our warfare are not carnal, but mighty through God to the pulling down of strong holds);* **Casting down imaginations, and every high thing that exalts itself against the knowledge of God, and bringing into captivity every thought to the obedience of Christ"**

--2 Corinthians 10:3-5 (KJV), emphasis added

Or, as the Amplified Version of the Bible translates it:

*"For though we walk in the flesh [as mortal men], we are not carrying on our [spiritual] warfare according to the flesh and using the weapons of man. The weapons of our warfare are not physical [weapons of flesh and blood]. Our weapons are divinely powerful for the destruction of fortresses.* **We are destroying sophisticated arguments and every exalted and proud thing that sets itself up against the [true] knowledge of God, and we are taking every thought and purpose captive to the obedience of Christ."**

--2 Corinthians 10:3-5

These three verses are jam-packed with information concerning spiritual warfare. They bring complete awareness to how we ought to fight and what exactly we are fighting! I will try to break this down in the simplest of terms:

In verse 3, we are reminded that although we live in human bodies made of flesh and blood, we are not fighting in a war that consists of another human body made of flesh and blood. This means there are no man-made weapons that can be used for this kind of fight!

In verse 4, we are told that since there are no physical weapons which can be used, we are given spiritual weapons that are from the Lord! This is done because **the Lord refuses to have us powerless, hopeless, and helpless on the earth!** All the help we need is here, and the Bible is the only book that tells us what is available to us and how to make full use of it on a daily basis.

We are also told that these weapons are powerful to assist in the destruction of fortresses, or strongholds. These are the grounds that the enemy is trying to establish within us. It is as if the devil is setting up camp within our mind, a place he can use as his base to execute wicked plans which are detrimental to us and to others, and can ultimately lead to our demise!

In verse 5, we are told that we can destroy sophisticated arguments. We need to recognize that these thoughts that will enter your mind are cleverly put together. These are thoughts and ideas are our enemy knows have worked for centuries in the past. These thoughts may seem to us like good ideas; this is because they cater to satisfying the desires of our sinful nature! The very same nature we are told needs to be put to death daily because it goes against God's will for our lives (Romans 8:13)!

It is good news indeed to know that these sophisticated arguments which are being raised can be destroyed! Sadly, in most people's lives, they are not being destroyed, but instead they are thriving and growing into strong feelings and desires … and before you know it:

> Adultery is committed.

> Drugs are used.

> Alcohol is abused.

- A house is burglarized.

- Pornography is watched.

- Some sort of sexual perversion is committed.

- A person hates another person because of their skin color, not realizing that we were all colored by God!

- A person's character is assassinated behind their back.

- A child is molested.

- A woman is raped.

- A person is assaulted.

- A person is murdered.

- A person commits suicide.

All because the reasoning and sophisticated arguments that came from Satan, our adversary, were never confronted, challenged, and removed! But you and I – and as many others as we can spread this news to – will no longer succumb to the devil's old bag of effective tricks!

**(Thank you, Lord, for opening our eyes and allowing us to clearly see the invisible world of spirits through our understanding of Your Word)**

Now, notice another brilliant thing which verse 5 tells us to do, which is part of the method of destroying these thoughts. It talks about, *"taking every thought captive."*

This means to literally stop the thought in its tracks and examine it. It is the equivalent of stopping a thirteen-year-old kid who broke into your home, grabbing him by the shirt, and asking "what are you doing here? How did you get into my house?" However, Paul goes on to say we should not just take that thought captive, but to make it line up in obedience to Christ Jesus. This means bringing that thought to the highest authority to see what He has to say about it. Only a person whose heart is right, open, and honest before God would even want to do this!

Most people will keep their thoughts to themselves, especially when they recognize they are bad! They do not want to share them out of fear of feeling guilt and shame! What they do not know, and what you now have to realize, is that **you are not every thought that enters your mind!** So, there is no need to feel guilt or shame when the thought comes to you; many times, it is merely an evil spirit fishing to see whether you will take the bait and fall for the lie!

When a new and strange thought suddenly comes to you, that does not make you one with the thought. Nor does it mean that you agree with such thoughts! You have the option of either agreeing or disagreeing, much like you are not responsible for someone breaking into your home, you are not responsible for every thought that pops into your mind. **You only become responsible for a thought once you agree with it**. As soon as you agree with that thought, you are guilty in the eyes of God of the act before you even commit it (Jeremiah 17:10)!

In fact, perhaps there have been times when you may have wanted to go and act upon a sinful thought, and God almighty has intervened and stopped you! Why did He do that? Because He loves you and although the enemy wants you dead, God wants to keep you alive and give you the abundant life which Jesus has promised you!

**You are Only as Strong as Your Foundation:**

Many people fight these battles in their minds on their own every day … and fail! Some may get a momentary victory, only to fail later at the 7th or 8th visitation of the thought! They then become frustrated and angry at themselves, and sometimes angry at God, accusing God of making them that way! They convince themselves that God is allowing them to fulfill their evil desires, something which their conscience tells them is wrong and should not be fulfilled, and they feel stuck!

The problem is they are in darkness, and the eyes of their understanding are closed, so they cannot see what they are up against! And when a person merely tries to resist evil thoughts on their own, it only lasts for a moment, because the devil can tell whether Christ dwells within that person.

All that is needed is a personal relationship with the Lord so their lives can be placed on a solid foundation! They need to receive His salvation which is being offered through faith in Christ Jesus! But they certainly cannot come up with this answer on their own. This is the reason more of us need to go out and spread the good News!

This is worth repeating: **the reason people fail is because they lack the right foundation to stand upon!** And without that foundation, you will not have the right power you need. You are only as strong as your foundation. Listen to what Jesus has to say about those who have a strong foundation and those who do not:

*"So, everyone who hears these words of Mine and acts on them, will be like a wise man [a far-sighted, practical, and sensible man] who built his house on the rock. And the rain fell, and the floods and torrents came, and the winds blew and slammed against that house; yet it did not fall, because it had been founded on the rock. And everyone who hears these words of Mine and does not do them, will be like a foolish (stupid) man who built his house on the sand. And the rain fell, and the floods and torrents came, and the winds blew and slammed against that house; and it fell--and great and complete was its fall."*

--Mathew 7:24-27

Listening to the Lord by obeying His Word causes your life to be established on the strongest foundation there is! It is a foundation that is strengthened by God Himself! Choosing this path enables the Lord to provide for us in every area of our lives, both in the spiritual and the physical aspects of our well- being. The Lord sees that you are making the best decisions that can be made by choosing to love Him and to obey His word!

He also knows this is something none of us can ever do on our own. So to those who submit to Him, He lovingly fills us with His Spirit to give us the power we need to live the life we cannot live by ourselves!

*"If you love me, keep my commandments. And I will pray to the Father, and he shall give you another Comforter, that he may abide with you forever. Even the Spirit of truth; whom the world cannot receive because it sees him not, neither knows him: but you know him; for he dwells with you and shall be in you. **I will not leave you comfortless: I will come to you.**"*

--John 14:15-18 (KJV/our version), emphasis added

And when Jesus said He would not leave them without comfort, but would come to them, He meant that through the presence of the Spirit of Truth, He will be with us as well!

Then later, He said this:

*"But you will receive power and ability when the Holy Spirit comes upon you; and you will be My witnesses [to tell people about Me] both in Jerusalem and in all Judea, and Samaria, and even to the ends of the earth."*

--Acts 1:8

Now that this power is in us, we must continue to fight. Only now, we are fighting with complete knowledge and

65

awareness of who we are up against and how they operate. And we are empowered to use the word of God as a sword to fight with!

**The Perfect Fight**:

Jesus, who had never committed sin of any kind, was tempted by Satan. The devil wanted to see if he could cause Jesus to sin against God by listening to and believing his lies. In essence, this was a rematch of the showdown between good and evil which took place in the Garden of Eden, as described in Genesis Chapter 3, where Eve was tempted and deceived. But Jesus would not fall for any of Satan's lies. As you read the story, you will see that each time the devil spoke a lie, Jesus replied with the truth … not once or twice, but all three times!

These are the same type of temptations that the enemy still uses on us today. Not the exact same words, or even the exact same enticements, but the exact same method of seeking to gain access to our minds and hearts.

The first area is the lust of the flesh, meaning the uncontrollable desire to want to please the flesh at all costs and by any means. But Jesus rejected the offer! He knew He would eat when the time was right:

*"And when the tempter came to him, he said, 'if you are the Son of God, command that these stones be made bread.' But he answered and said, **'it is written, Man shall not live by bread alone, but by every word that proceeds out of the mouth of God.**"*

--Mathew 4:3-4 (KJV), emphasis added

The second area was the pride of life, meaning to arrogantly boast of one's power and fame to look and feel good in front of others; To appear to even be better than others; To merely show other people the authority you have for vain reasons. But Jesus did not fall for that either, because He was confident in who He was!

*"... 'If you are the Son of God, cast yourself down; for it is written, He shall give his angels charge concerning thee, and in their hands, they shall bear you up, lest at any time you dash your foot against a stone.'* Jesus said to him, **'It is written again, you shall not tempt the Lord your God.'"**

--Matthew 4:6-7 (KJV), emphasis added

Finally, the devil tempted Him with the most successful means of temptation which most human beings fall for: Riches. The lust of the eyes ... but again, Jesus did not fall for this! He knew He owned the world and that all the kingdoms of the earth were already His!

*"Again, the devil took him up into an exceeding high mountain, and showed him all the kingdoms of the world, and the glory of them. And said to him, 'all these things will I give you, if you will fall down and worship me.'* Then Jesus said to him, **'get away, Satan: for it is written, you shall worship the Lord your God, and him only shall you serve.'"**

-- Mathew 4:8-10 (author's interpretation)

Always remember to believe and to say what the Lord Himself has said about you. This way, you will always have His support to back you up.

> ➢ Say what you know God wants for your life.

> ➢ Say what God loves and what God hates.

> ➢ Say what you know is written in the Word of God.

This is the reason why you must set time apart daily to read His word, that you might know His heart and fuel your mind with the purity and potency of His powerful words. Set times to just **turn the TV off** and spend some time in prayer and the reading of His word, because His word will continue to renew your mind and change the way you think and respond. It will even change how you see yourself and respond to others! You will find the courage and strength you need to overcome everything the enemy can throw at you, because you now have greater power and abilities to do greater things through Him.

*"Little children (believers, dear ones), you are of God and you belong to Him and have [already] overcome them [the agents of the antichrist]; because He who is in you is greater than he (Satan) who is in the world [of sinful mankind]."*

--1 John 4:4

**You Will Win the Fight:**

Your life will go in the direction of the words you believe and you say out of your mouth! This is your version of Jesus' confrontation with the devil in Matthew 4:

*"Devil, you are a liar! I am not taking my life! No matter how bad things may seem, I know that God did not create me and give me life, just so that I can one day take my own life!"*

*"Devil, you are a liar and I refuse to believe you!"*

*"If God wants me dead, He knows exactly how to take my life And He does not need my help!"*

--see Deuteronomy 32:39

*"Devil, you are a Liar! God has a perfect plan for my life!"*

*"A plan for good and not for evil,*

*to give me an expected end!"*

--see Jeremiah 29:11

*"Devil you are a liar! God desires that I would prosper and be in good health! He even wants my heart and mind to prosper. He wants nothing but good for my life! Therefore, get away from me devil, I have a good God to love and to serve! I will bring my problems to the Lord and He will help me with all of them!"*

--see 3 John 1:2 & 1 Peter 5:7

*"Devil you are a Liar! Take your own life!"*

*"Jesus said that He came that I should have life and have it more abundantly! So, if He wants me to have abundant life, what right do I – or anyone else have – to take my life?"*

*"Again, devil, you are a liar and the father of Lies!"*

*"Take your own life! I am going to live the abundant life that Christ Jesus wants me to live!"*

*"And I choose to honor Him with my life!"*

--see John 10:10 & John 8:44

Boldly making these statements (out loud or to yourself) tells the enemy that you are aware of who he is and what he's up to he will flee (James 4:7). Because he is known by you he will leave and find someone else. But he will come back in the future to check and see if your faith is still in God!

Speak the Word and it will be like a sword coming out of your mouth

# Chapter 7

# It Makes No Sense!

Now, I would like to speak with you from a sensible point of view, from one human being to another. And please note that this is coming from a man who genuinely loves and cares about you and your well-being. I want to give you ten reasons why suicide makes no sense:

**It Makes No Sense:**

1.      God created you to live! And why would He breathe life into you, only to turn around and tell you to take your life! He would not do this, Because it is not His desire. If He wanted to take your life, He knows exactly how to do it! He does not need your help or anyone else's.

--see Deuteronomy 32:39.

2.      The only one that wants you to commit suicide is the devil, who does not care about any human being. So why should you or anyone else give him what he wants, and not give God what he wants? That makes no sense!

3.      It would mean that you chose to believe the devil who is the father of lies ... who comes to kill, steal, and destroy, as opposed to Jesus who is the Truth, who came to give us life and give it to us more abundantly! So that would mean that you left earth listening to the devil.

4.	It would also mean the very last thing you did on this earth was break one of God's Ten Commandments, namely "thou shall not kill," so how in the world could that be rewarded on the other side of this life?

5.	It only makes matters worse! Nothing at all gets better for you or for the family members you leave behind. Just check out the outcome of those whose family members committed suicide. Not only are they hurt, but many are so traumatized by the loss of that person that it becomes hard for them to function normally. And every time they think of the fact that their family member killed themselves, it just refreshes the pain and agony … it is like torturing your family for the rest of their lives!

6.	If your sense of hopelessness is stemming from being ostracized, made fun of, or not welcomed, those are behavior traits that are coming from people who are led by the devil and his demons … people who are plain evil! People who are possibly on their way to hell. People who you should stay away from to begin with. So why in the world would you give them what they want? That amounts to rewarding your enemy. That makes no sense! If anything, continue to live and become something great, and they will wish they were your friend. That is how you deal with that crowd!

7.	If there is a secret sinful struggle you have and you are too ashamed to talk to anyone about it, take your burdens to the Lord! He can handle it! He will not embarrass you! He knows what you are going through, and He knows exactly how you got there! Your sinful ways did not take him by surprise. He knew beforehand that you would do those things, and all He is asking you to do now is to turn from your wicked ways and cry out and submit to Him! And not only will He forgive you, but He is offering you the power to help you! That is a win-win situation!

8.    If you have already committed the worse sin imaginable, it did not take God by surprise! There is still an opportunity God is giving you to repent and ask for forgiveness! It was not an unforgivable act! There is mercy at His throne that is available and waiting for you to take advantage of right now! And the reason why He is making it available for you is because He loves you!

9.    Suicide is not your best option! Regardless of the reason that you are considering it, let me give you your best option. Since death by suicide is the issue, we are discussing the thoughts that are coming to your mind. Here is another death that you can commit … a death that is safe for you and for everyone in your life … a death that will slam the door in the face of the devil and cause him to be angry that he could not succeed at destroying you … a death that is pleasing in the eyes of God!

Why not just die to yourself, meaning your ways? Your thoughts? Your desires? Your goals and your agenda? There is nothing wrong with hating who you have become and all your ways, because Jesus said that to obtain the life which He wants us to have, we must hate the life we are leaving behind!

*"If any man come to me, and hate not his father, and mother, and wife, and children, and brothers, and sisters, yes and his own life also, he cannot be my disciple."*

--Luke 14:26

Fall on your knees and cry out to God, and say:

*"Lord, today I die to myself and to all of my ways!*

*Give me a brand, new life and live this new life through me!*

*I am completely yours. In Jesus name I pray!*

10.     Suicide arrogantly and defiantly tells God He cannot have His way with the life He created in you! A life which is possible to offer to Him, but you are choosing not to do so! I pray you have reconsidered your thoughts concerning suicide, or, if you were just reading this to help others, you have come away with a better understanding of how to enlighten others who are struggling with the real notion of ending their lives.

11.   My Last reason I want to leave you with is this! God Loves you and has demonstrated His love for you in many ways. Such as through Creation itself and through providing Salvation through Jesus so you can be forgiven for your sins and spend eternity with Him! And yes there are many other ways God has shown you His love but the one that also hits me as well as you is the fact that He led me to write you this book in yet another attempt to reach

out to you and prevent you from doing something that He doesn't want you to do! That's Love!

Take advantage of His love and give Him what He wants and that is a beautiful intimate Father and Child Relationship with You!

I pray that a new perspective springs forth within your soul ... and that the devil is totally removed from your life as He is further exposed as being the father of lies!

I also pray you would be so strengthened by your newfound relationship with Jesus you would become a spokesperson for the fight against these 100% preventable and senseless acts of suicide.

Father, I pray that the reader of this book be totally delivered from all bondages of lies, both known and unknown! And that as they submit their lives to You, they would be filled with your joy and peace that surpasses all their human understanding! And that You would lead them by Your Spirit in the way which You would have them go, and that You would place the right people in their lives and allow them to be at peace with the people that they need to be removed from! And finally, that You would be totally glorified and honored by the life that they will now live!

**I Thank you in advance for answering my prayers!**

**In Christ Jesus' name, I pray!**

\*     \*     \*

Please begin to read the Word of God daily!

Start with the book of St John in the New Testament and pay close attention to all the words of Jesus!

Get involved in a Bible-believing church where you sense the love of God, where people make mention of the Holy Spirit of God and are not ashamed to mention the name and authority of Jesus Christ! These are some of the characteristics of a good, sound church.

**Remember that there is way more power available through Jesus Christ to help you than the powers of darkness that can harm you!**

Be blessed, take care, and enjoy your new life!

# "Says Who?"

Suicide!!?
Throw in the towel cause you can't seem to breakthrough?
Terminate the life that God almighty gave you?
Says who?
And are they taking their lives too!?

Who was given the right to appraise you!
And turn around and devalue who God made you?

Just because you failed doesn't mean you're a failure!
You may have made some mistakes,
But you're not a mistake!
Because you were made by God
And GOD DOESN'T MAKE MISTAKES!

You've tried to change for people,
And that's where the road ends.
Your efforts never paid off,
'cause you need to change your friends!

Who said that you can't make it?
And there's nothing you can do!
You believe your life is hopeless,
But the question is "Says Who?"

Your past does not define you,
Those voices are not true!
The truth just needs to take its place,
with the will inside of you!

So, if you think there's no solution,
As all hope just keeps on crashing,
Jesus is the answer,
to the problems that you're having.

Your thoughts have been polluted,
And sin was executed!
But His word is the cure,
To make your thinking pure!

Bring your burdens to the Lord,
There's nothing you can't tell Him.
cause If God wants to take your life,
He doesn't need you to help him.

So, if you made some Bad decisions,
It doesn't mean your life is through.
There is power to make you new!
And to remove demons that don't belong in you!

He created you to live!
And when you sin and confess,
There is Mercy to forgive!

And when you feel like giving up,
There is grace to help you through!
And when you feel like no one cares,
He'll put His love inside of you!

And bring people in your life,
who will love you just for you!
Because there's nothing that God almighty can not do!

So, die to your own agenda,
Die to the lust of the flesh.

Ask God for His Spirit,
That your weary soul rest!

He's given you a lot,
And there's more He wants to give.

So, tell the devil he's a liar,
God ordained for you to live!

Yes, tell the devil to take his own life,
God ordained for you to live!

The End


Visit our website at:

www.TheDeathofSuicide.com
Youtube: TheDeathofSuicide (For the
Poem "Says Who?" recited)

To request speaking engagements, send an
email to:

poeticseer@yahoo.com

# Acknowledgements

I want to thank my extremely supportive family and friends.


And I must certainly thank my Lord, Jesus Christ, for giving me the wisdom and guidance to write and release this book!

# About the author

MARK B. ROGERS is an author, poet, public speaker, and advocate of the truth!  With a deep love and concern for all human beings, he is presently on a mission to drastically reduce the senseless and 100% preventable deaths of suicide!

Other books by Mark B. Rogers

"WHAT IF YOU'RE WRONG?"

"30 PIECES OF SILVER"

NO MORE SEXUAL CONFUSION

YOU'RE BEAUTIFUL AND I CAN PROVE IT

WHO ARE YOU?

AVAILABLE ON AMAZON BOOKS , APPLE IBOOKS AND GOOGLE BOOKS.

COMING SOON: "HIJACKED" &

"SPIRITUAL WARFARE, ANGELS & DEMONS

FOR SPEAKING ENGAGEMENTS EMAIL: \

POETICSEER@YAHOO.COM

# VISIT OUR WEBSITE

# WWW.MAKEYOUFREE.ORG

www.ingramcontent.com/pod-product-compliance
Lightning Source LLC
Chambersburg PA
CBHW071926020426
42331CB00010B/2744